7 NOTABLE IMPACT OF SOCIAL MEDIA ON POLITICS.

Outlining the benefits and drawbacks.

By

JOHN DAVIDSON

TABLE OF CONTENT

ABOUT THE AUTHOR

INTRODUCTION

TABLE OF CONTENTS

Chapter 7:
The Role of Regulation in Social Media

Conclusion:

JOHN DAVIDSON is a political writer who writes both fiction and nonfiction works.an investigative reporter who regularly writes on trending politics, government and history.he is one of the most influential public intellectuals in the world and one of the most often cited scholarship modern history.

Introduction:

Social media has become an essential part of our daily lives, altering how we interact with one another and with the world around us. Its impact goes far beyond our social circles and has had a significant impact on politics. The rise of social media has given politicians and political campaigns new opportunities and challenges. It has provided a platform for people to express themselves, mobilize others, and form movements. However, it has also been used to disseminate misinformation, spread propaganda, and sway elections. This paper will investigate the impact of social media on politics, including its benefits and drawbacks, its role in shaping public opinion, the use of social media by politicians, and its impact on democracy.

Chapter 1:

The Influence of Social Media on Public Opinion.

Social media has emerged as a potent tool for influencing public opinion. It enables people to express their opinions and participate in political debates in previously impossible ways. People can use social media platforms such as Twitter, Facebook, and Instagram to share news, opinions, and political views with their friends, family, and followers. This has resulted in the formation of echo chambers, in which people are only exposed to views that reinforce their beliefs, resulting in a polarized political climate.

Chapter 2:

Politicians' Use of Social Media.

Politicians have also embraced social media as a means of communicating with voters. It has enabled them to communicate directly with their constituents, bypassing traditional media outlets. This has allowed politicians to establish a more personal connection with their supporters and to present their views and policies unfiltered.

Politicians can also use social media to raise funds and mobilize supporters for their campaigns.

CHAPTER 3

The Rise of Digital Campaigning

The rise of social media has also increased digital campaigning. Political campaigns are now using social media to send tailored messages to specific groups of voters. This has increased the effectiveness of political advertising and allowed campaigns to reach a larger audience. Candidates can also use social media to spread their message without relying on traditional media outlets.

CHAPTER 4

The Impact of Social Media on Elections

Elections have been significantly influenced by social media. It has enabled candidates to reach a larger audience and has made mobilizing supporters easier. Social media, on the other hand, has been used to spread disinformation, propaganda, and influence elections. Fake news stories and conspiracy theories have spread on social media, polarizing the political landscape and undermining trust in democratic institutions.

CHAPTER 5

The Impact of Social Media on Political Activism

Political activism has also been greatly influenced by social media. It has provided a platform for people to express their opinions and mobilize others around political causes. Protests, marches, and other forms of political action have been organized using social media. As a result, new movements such as Black

Lives Matter and #MeToo have emerged.

CHAPTER 6

Social Media and the Future of Democracy

The rise of social media has posed new challenges to democracy. Disinformation and propaganda have eroded trust in democratic institutions, and the polarized political environment has made it more difficult to find common ground. However, social media has provided people with a platform to express their opinions and engage in political debates, which can aid in the promotion of democratic values. The future of democracy will be determined by how we respond to the challenges posed by social media and how we use it to promote democratic values.

Chapter 7:

The Role of Regulation in Social Media

The impact of social media on politics has prompted calls for government regulation. Concerns have been raised about the spread of misinformation, foreign actors using social media to interfere in elections, and the polarized political climate. Regulation, by requiring a social response, could help to address these issues.

Conclusion:

Social media has altered the political landscape in ways unimaginable just a few decades ago. It has altered how political parties and candidates interact with voters, how political messages are crafted and communicated, and how people participate in the political process. While social media has resulted in many positive changes, it has also increased political polarization and reduced civil discourse. As we move forward, it is critical to understand the impact of social media on politics and consider how we can use its power for good.

www.ingramcontent.com/pod-product-compliance
Lightning Source LLC
Chambersburg PA
CBHW071130220526
45467CB00004B/2111